# Dalai Lama

(The Practice of Buddhism)

*Lessons for Happiness,
Fulfillment, Meaning, Inspiration
and Living*

# Table of Contents

Introduction

Chapter 1: Buddhism Explained

Chapter 2: The Buddha

Chapter 3: The Dalai Lama

Chapter 4: Love And Compassion

Chapter 5: Meditation and Techniques

Chapter 6: Selflessness (and how it applies to the modern world)

Chapter 7: Buddhist Traditions

Chapter 8: Prayer and Rituals

Chapter 9: Impermanence

Chapter 10: Happiness, Fulfillment and Meaning

Chapter 11: Karma

Chapter 12: Dharma (Limited Time BONUS Chapter)

Chapter 13: Getting Started with Buddhism

Chapter 14: Further Resources

Conclusion

# Introduction

Most of us go through our lives looking for more meaning. Whether you are a top executive or a mom working from home, the idea that there simply has to be more to life must have occurred to you at one time or another.

Some people are lucky and find the right formula for happiness fairly early on in life. For the rest, finding their bliss can entail a life long struggle, and may even span the course of several lifetimes.

There are so many different experts out there, all with their own way to help you to lead a fulfilling life. This leads to a lot of confusion. Whose advice do you follow? Whose advice do you ignore?

Spirituality is one area that most experts agree upon - the idea that there is a higher state that can be achieved, a more perfect version of ourselves - whether this is a particular God or even just within ourselves. Experts agree that we need to take note of the spiritual aspect of our lives or they will never be completely fulfilled.

The key here is that you need to find a spiritual belief system that resonates with you. Something that you can really understand and take to heart. And this means finding out what other belief systems there are out there and how much sense they make to you personally.

It could also mean changing from the belief system of your parents and this might be scary for you. What you need to remember though is that this is about your life and happiness. At the end of the day, your family will want you to do what is right for you.

For me personally, this was a journey that took over twenty years and I still cannot say that it is completely over. Who knows, in ten years time, a different belief system may make more sense to me and I may have to make adjustments accordingly.

One thing that I have noticed during my studies is that many religions, whilst they look very different on the surface, have similar underlying belief systems.

The main key with all religions appears to practice active compassion and to really try to understand and care for our fellow man.

If you want happiness, fulfillment, meaning and inspiration, the simple truth is that you are the only person that is able to make that happen. You are the one who will have to do the heavy lifting, no one can do it for you.

In this book, I am going to give you an overview of Buddhism and some important life lessons. Use what makes sense to you and ignore the rest.

# Chapter 1: Buddhism Explained

## A Quick Overview Of Buddhism

I am sure that you have heard the phrase, "bad karma" at one time or another. You may even have told someone that karma was going to get them. Karma is an important concept in Buddhism and probably one element of the Buddhist belief system that most people have heard about.

The truth is though that karma is really only one element of a complex belief system and that most of us misunderstand how it works anyway.

Buddhism is not a religion so much as a philosophy of living. It is based on the teachings of the Buddha - a simple man who was never actually deified. There is no actual God or Goddess to worship in Buddhism, you simply work towards becoming an enlightened individual and reach Nirvana.

This personal journey can take many lifetimes to accomplish and can be a difficult path to follow. To be truly enlightened is to see the world and everything in it as it really is, without illusions. To understand that humans are higher beings in their own right and that they have the capability, above all other creatures on earth, to achieve enlightenment.

## The Buddha

The Buddha was revered as an enlightened man, but a man nonetheless. The Buddha left teachings for his followers on how to achieve the same level of enlightenment. In essence, Buddhists believe that each person can find the divine in themselves through living a moral life of compassion and mindfulness.

As a result, there are no Gods or Goddesses in Buddhism. You and you alone are responsible for your progress through life and how happy you are.

## Achieving Enlightenment and Reaching Nirvana

As mentioned above, achieving enlightenment is the ultimate goal for those practising Buddhism. This is done through learning several lessons, possibly over several different lifetimes. Each lesson brings you one step closer to understanding everything.

The Buddha was considered an enlightened being and if you wish to achieve the same degree of enlightenment, you need to follow the steps he laid out for you. These include moral action and thought, being mindful and practising meditation.

Actions that you take in this life will influence what your next incarnations will be like - that is where karma comes in - and you will either progress towards Nirvana or hit a bit of a roadblock, meaning that you will need to work harder towards creating good karma for yourself.

## Nirvana

Nirvana is achieved when all suffering is ended. According to the basic tenets of Buddhism, suffering stems from desire. This means that if you can eliminate desire from your life, you can achieve Nirvana.

The phrase, "Heaven on Earth" comes to mind here - Nirvana is something that everyone is able to achieve in their lives. It is not a separate place at all.

Essentially, to achieve a true state of Nirvana, you need to get to a place where you feel no desire whatsoever. No hunger, no love, no hate, etc. This allows you to truly exist in the moment.

Imagine for a moment that you did not want that new car, or new house, etc. If you were truly living in the moment, you wouldn't want these things and so you would not have desires. Desires, by their nature, imply lack.

That means that most of us go to work every day because we feel in our core that we are lacking something. Scary thought, isn't it?

## Rebirth

There is no separate heaven in the Buddhist faith - you are born, learn the soul lessons that you were put on earth for and die. You are then reborn again, in order that you can continue working towards enlightenment. When you are an enlightened being, you can choose to end the cycle or not, depending on what you want to do.

## To Suffer or Not to Suffer

Buddhists do not recognize the concept of sin in the same way that Christians do. You can, essentially, do whatever you want. What does happen though is that all your actions are weighed as moral or immoral.

When you die, there is no heaven or hell to go to. You are simply reborn into a new life. If you did a lot of bad things in your previous life, you can expect to suffer in the next one. You could end up being raised in poverty, as a slave, or even as an animal.

It is not just the actions that you take but also your intentions that come into play here. Perhaps you stole a loaf of bread to feed your family - stealing is considered wrong but your intentions were good so it is more likely to fall on the positive side of the scale.

On the other hand, perhaps you stole the latest fashion watch so that you could brag to your friends. That is also wrong and the reason behind it is too so it falls on the negative side of the scale.

In Buddhism, things are not always black and white.

# Chapter 2: The Buddha

## Understanding Siddhartha - An Extra-Ordinary Man

A Buddha is an enlightened and holy person and there have been several throughout the course of history. In essence, anyone could become a Buddha as long as they become enlightened. The person that we refer to as the Buddha, Siddhartha, was one such person and the one credited with laying out the instructions that are now considered the tenets of Buddhism.

Siddhartha Gautama was a royal prince born in the foothills of the Himalayas, in the Kingdom of Shakya, around about 600 years before the birth of Christ. The name "Siddhartha" means "every wish fulfilled" as he was the only son and heir born to the couple.

Shortly after the baby was born, the king held a feast and invited a number of high ranking priests to come and tell him what the future held for Siddhartha.

## A Great Ruler or Great Spiritual Teacher?

According to many of these priests, there were two distinct possibilities - Siddhartha could lead a life of luxury and stay at the palace or he could leave the palace and lead a life of hardships.

If he chose the former, he would become a great ruler; if he chose the latter, he would become a great spiritual teacher.

Kondanna, one of the priests, had no doubt that the prince would become a great spiritual teacher and pointed out that there would be four signs that would put the prince on this path.

## Guess What the King Chose

The king naturally wanted his son to be his successor and so gave the prince everything he wanted. He was protected from seeing anything bad in life and encouraged the prince to stay within the walls of the palace.

When Siddhartha did go outside the palace, the king made sure that everything looked perfect, hiding anything that could denote misery or suffering.

## The Four Signs

The signs that preceded Siddhartha's journey to enlightenment, as laid out by Kondanna all occurred during visits to the outside world. It was during these four visits that Siddhartha learned about aging, illness, death and asceticism. All of these left a mark on the prince and he started to see the world as full of suffering as opposed to being full of luxury.

## Siddhartha's Marriage

Siddhartha got married at the age of 16 to Yasodhara, rumored to be the most beautiful woman in the kingdom. His pampered life continued until he was 21 and his wife fell pregnant.

It was after the birth of his son that Siddhartha decided to leave his life of luxury behind. He snuck out of the palace and became a monk. He made a vow to lead a life free of attachments and to try and save every single being from suffering.

## A Moderate Path

At the time, asceticism was recognised as the true path to becoming enlightened. It was believed that suffering sufficiently in this life would allow you to negate any bad karma accumulated or allow you to end the cycle of rebirth.

After a while as an ascetic, Siddhartha became annoyed as he realized that he might die as a result of this lifestyle without getting closer to enlightenment.

From then on, he practised a more moderate approach - neither completely denying himself or completely indulging himself either.

He found that mindfulness was a more important lesson - that one has to mindful of everything one does.

Through practising mindfulness and meditation, he began to realize that everything was interconnected. He also realized that nothing was permanent - time passes, everything dies - all that matters is the moment that you are living in. Things do not matter.

# Chapter 3: The Dalai Lama
## Tibet's Spiritual Leader

Tibetan Buddhism is a little different from the traditional school of Buddhism in that they believe that not only can every person become a Buddha, but also that there are a good number of Buddhas in the world. That said, Siddhartha is considered to be the main Buddha, or most important, Buddha of this time period.

There are several different traditions within Tibetan Buddhism but all of them center around the belief that compassion is paramount - anyone can achieve enlightenment and everyone should help others on the path to becoming enlightened.

## The Dalai Lama

The closest English translation for Dalai Lama is "Ocean of Wisdom". The Dalai Lama is the spiritual leader of Tibet and is considered an incarnation of Avalokitehvara and so is the embodiment of compassion.

The Dalai Lama is not a leadership position in the sense that we understand it to be. You cannot aspire to the position, you have to be born into it. Basically, when the current Dalai Lama dies, his spirit is reborn into a new body.

The government and people of Tibet then search for this incarnation of the Dalai Lama. If it is believed that the right person has been found, a selection of items are placed in front of the candidate, including items that belonged to the late Dalai Lama. Should the candidate recognize their possessions, they are confirmed as the new Dalai Lama.

In spirit, therefore, the last 14 Dalai Lamas have all been the same person.

## His Holiness, Tenzin Gyatso

The current Dalai Lama, Tenzin Gyatso, was born in the Amdo province of Tibet in 1935. The previous Dalai Lama had died just two years prior to this and it is said that his head moved mysteriously toward the Amdo province whilst his body was sitting in state.

Tenzin was identified at the age of 3 and is said to have recognized some of the monks that came to test him. When presented with the choice of objects, he is said to have straight away claimed objects belonging to the previous Dalai Lama as being his own.

He was taken away from his family at that stage in order to begin his training. At the age of 15 he was formally made ruler of Tibet.

He stayed in Tibet trying to garner support to fight off Chinese invaders until 1959 when he went into exile.

To this day, China claims ownership of this mountain kingdom, despite the claims of the native Tibetan people.

# Chapter 4: Love And Compassion

## The Path to Enlightenment

Whilst it is not hard for most of us in the Western world to understand the idea that compassion is key in making our life more fulfilling, the idea that we should love every living being unconditionally can be a little harder to accept. We get so caught up in little slights and feuds and how others have wronged us that we tend to forget that they have also taught us valuable lessons.

## Every Person is a Teacher

Every person that you come across in your life is there for a reason. They are there to teach you something. Think about it for a minute - the lessons may not have been pleasant to learn, but they were lessons none the less.

I used to work with a woman that I believed was manipulative and really nasty. She made my life at work hell and so I resigned. Imagine my surprise when I encountered a similar person at the next place I worked, and again at a place I worked at a few years later.

Clearly one of my life lessons was learning how to deal with this type of person. It took a while, but eventually I learned that it was not these women that had the problem at all - I knew what type of people they were and I let their behavior get to me, I let it make me feel unhappy. I since learned some coping techniques and now I can deal with them if need be.

Every person is a teacher - no matter how hard the lesson that they are teaching is.

I now endeavour to love and understand them. I'm not going to lie to you, I had a lot of hate in my heart for that first woman and it took me a long time to let go of that. In fact, it took running into a similar person at two other jobs to understand that I was the one that needed to change.

Now I am thankful for the lesson and can look back at all of these women without rancour - I simply don't care about how they behaved anymore.

## You Have More Power Than You Think

Another lesson that I learned from that woman was that everything passes. I worked under her for 7 years and it felt like it was my whole life. When I got out of that situation, I realized that it wasn't my whole life and that everything passed when its time was done.

Was my life better? Not really because I would play back incidents with this woman in my mind over and over again. I was physically free of the situation but not mentally free of it.

And there is a basic truth that is found in Buddhism - your mind creates its own heaven or hell. In my mind, I was still trapped in that situation, I needed to get over it in order to have a happier life.

I began to realize that I was acting from a desire to be proven right, to be vindicated. It was quickly apparent that I had to set aside my own ego in order to be able to get to develop some deeper understanding of her behaviour.

Looking at it more objectively, I began to realize that she clearly had a very poor self-esteem. In her mind, I was the threat. She herself was not a happy person. I actually began to feel more compassion towards her - after all, she was clearly a damaged person herself.

I began to think about the way I had treated her and the way I had reacted to her actions and, I must be honest, there were times that I did not like what I saw. I had also done things that I was not proud of.

Now, would treating her with compassion have made a big difference to the way she treated me? Would loving her and all her faults unconditionally made her behavior more reasonable?

Probably not, but it would have been more in keeping with the person that I wanted to be. I would have been able to look back without regret on that section of my life.

## Letting Go of Ego

I have given you a glimpse into my personal story. The reason that I was able to act as I did was because I was able to step back from my own ego.

Buddhists believe that you can never be truly happy unless you are selfless and that, in order to be truly selfless, you need to let go of the ego.

Being able to love others unconditionally is the ultimate proof that you have let go of your ego because it means that you no longer judge them in terms of your own personal beliefs and values.

Ultimately, we are all essentially the same, not one of us is truly more important than any of the others. We are all interconnected and it is our duty to help our fellow human beings.

Treating people with compassion comes naturally to a lot of us, it is almost instinctive - we all want to help.

Treating everyone with unconditional love is harder, at least to start with, it means admitting that perhaps you do not have all the right answers. That there could be other values and beliefs out there that are just as right as your own.

Ego is what gets in the way of loving others unconditionally and thus is gets in the way of you achieving enlightenment.

Is it really worthwhile to bolster your ego at the cost of true happiness?

# Chapter 5: Meditation and Techniques

## Learning How To Still Your Mind

I, for one, initially battled to quiet my mind enough to meditate. No matter how much chanting I did, I never did manage to still my mind completely. It took a while and trying a whole lot of different techniques but eventually I found a way that worked for me. I encourage you to try the different techniques in this chapter until you find one that works for you.

Buddhists believe that meditation is one way for you to learn about your true nature and so help you reach Nirvana. The quieting of the mind gives you a chance to see through the various illusions in life, to help to teach you about the impermanence of the moment and to create a calmer and more focused you.

## How Long to Meditate For

Ideally speaking, you should aim for 20 - 25 minutes of meditation a day. If you are just starting out, or if that sounds like too much for you, commit to at least 5 minutes a day until you get the hang of it. Once you start seeing the benefits in terms of stress reduction, etc. you will automatically want to spend more time meditating.

## What You Need

In most cases, you really do not need anything. If you are sitting on the floor, a cushion or mat might help you to feel more comfortable. The key is that your body should feel comfortable so that you can quiet your mind completely.

You want to be able to sit in the same position without developing cramping or any aches and pains that might interfere with your concentration.

I also find that setting a timer is useful. When I first started out, I did not do this and kept get worried that I would run late. This made it a lot harder to concentrate. If this is a fear for you, get a timer.

A timer can be a little bit of a shocking way to bring your focus back to the real world so do try and set the alert to some sort of soothing music or gentler tone if you can. When the timer goes off, respond to it gently - there is no need to jump up the minute it goes off. Give yourself some time to regain your focus.

Some people use incense as a kind of timer - when the incense goes out, it means that the time is up.

Prayer beads can be useful for keeping track of the number of repetitions of a chant/ prayer you have made.

As time goes on, you will be able to gauge for yourself how long you have been meditating for.

One thing you do need to make sure of is that you are wearing comfortable clothes. You want nothing that exerts pressure on your body.

## Your Posture

Traditionally the Lotus position is most popular. You sit on the floor with your legs and feet drawn up close to the body and crossed - with the bottom foot touching your butt and the top foot resting in the crook of your knee.

Beginners often battle to completely cross their legs so, if this is a problem for you, sit with your legs uncrossed but drawn up close to your body.

If getting down to, or up from, the floor is a problem, sit in a chair and ensure that your feet are flat against the ground.

Keep your back straight, with shoulders back so that your breathing is unrestricted. Rest your palms lightly on your knees.

## Quiet Time

Choose a time of the day when you are least likely to be disturbed. Switch off your phone and let your family know that you need some quiet time for the next few minutes.

Now that you have the basics ready, it is time to meditate.

## Shamatha Meditation

In this form of meditation, you focus on just one thing - it can be the sound of your breath or perhaps the sound of water dripping. If you are a beginner at meditation, this can be a great way to help drown out all the chatter. It requires no great skill or concentration.

Just concentrate on the sound or viewpoint that you have chosen and, if you find your mind wandering, gently nudge it back to concentrating on the chosen sound or viewpoint again.

One meditation in this line that I find useful is to count your breathing - breath in slowly to a count of four, hold for a count of four and then breathe out for a count of four. Listen to each breath and concentrate on counting. It is very effective at calming your mind.

You can also choose to meditate with your eyes open and concentrate on one particular point. This could be a spot on the wall or possibly the flame of the candle. The idea is to really look at what you have chosen and to think of nothing else at all.

## Vipashyana Meditation

If you are battling to clear your mind of all thought, an alternative is to concentrate on the thoughts themselves. Analyze the thought and let it pass without judgement. Perhaps, "The dogs are barking" as opposed to "The dogs are barking because they are so naughty."

The idea here is to realize that your brain is going to keep on thinking. You want to eventually work to a position where you are studying your thoughts in much the same way as a third party would - dispassionately and out of interest.

## Compassionate Meditation

This one does take a bit more practise but it can help to create a happier you. Basically you adopt simple, gentle affirmations, envision them and repeat them. Start by thinking these thoughts for yourself and then meditate for others as well. For example, you might start with, "May I be happy" and visualize yourself being happy and then move onto your best friend - "May Sarah be happy" before visualizing Sarah as being happy.

## Chanting

Chanting a mantra during meditation can help to really focus the mind. The sound vibrations can also be healing in and of themselves.

Try chanting, "Om" now - see how the sound resonates? Even though you are concentrating on reading this, chanting "Om" puts the book out of your mind for a second.

You can research mantras on the Internet or make up your own - the choice is yours.

Many people use different sounds to represent the different chakras in the body. It is thought that using the right sound for an unbalanced chakra can help to bring it back into balance.

When starting out, choose a simple mantra that is easy to repeat. If you need to think about what the words are, you are defeating the whole object of the exercise.

## A Walking Meditation

Walking during meditation can be an extremely useful way of getting some exercise and shutting off the mind as well. Walking meditation is slow and steady - concentrate on your steps and your breathing. Breathe in deeply as you step forward. Step again as you breath out slowly.

An alternative walking meditation is to walk a meditation labyrinth. This is slightly different to a maze in that you cannot get lost - all you do is to follow the path. The design is usually so intricate that your rational mind gives up trying to figure out where you are going and becomes a lot calmer.

## Mindfulness

For some people, the idea of sitting quietly for a few minutes concentrating on their breathing or chanting has no appeal whatsoever. If you are one of these people, you can something a little different, that works just as well.

You can do this when you are dusting the bookshelf, watering the garden or filing at work. All that you need to do is to concentrate completely on the task at hand.

## Make Meditation Work for You

It is important to keep trying until you find a way to get meditation to work for you. Perhaps it means getting up earlier in the morning, perhaps it means watching less TV at night. With the range of options presented, there is really no reason why you should not be able to include a meditation session in your daily schedule.

# Chapter 6: Selflessness (and how it applies to the modern world)

## How to Be Selfless In A World That Does Not Care

It seems that the current social culture is becoming a very selfish one - open up a magazine and you are bound to find something about getting more "me-time" or maximising your chances of success.

Perhaps it's not just society's fault though. We have generally become a more rushed and busy nation. It is not uncommon to work 14 hour days now and so it really isn't that much of a surprise that we are becoming more selfish. After all, when our leisure time is precious, we really don't think that we have time to be truly selfless.

## One Kind Act a Day

No matter how busy you are, there is no way that you do not have the time for 1 act of kindness a day. It doesn't have to be anything big - how about smiling at the cashier when she's packing your groceries, or asking her how her day has been going?

When you start looking for opportunities to be kind every day, it is amazing how many you find. Most will cost you nothing at all, some will cost a little bit of time. All will help to renew your soul and help to make you a nicer, kinder person. Your act of kindness could make that person's day or maybe even prompt them to be kind to others as well.

And that is how selflessness can start - from something as small as smiling at a stranger.

## Being Selfless

As we read earlier, being selfless is an important belief in Buddhism. We need to start losing our egos and practising unconditional love and compassion. Selflessness can help us to accomplish that.

Being selfless means that you are doing things for others, for no other reason than you want to help. You will not be getting any kind of material reward for these actions and are doing something that most likely will not help you to advance in terms of work goals or in the eyes of your colleagues or family. This is done just for someone else, not to stroke your own ego.

# Chapter 7: Buddhist Traditions

## The Importance of Tradition

Contrary to popular belief, tradition is not as important in Buddhist culture as you might think. The Buddha himself said that one should not simply believe that something is right and correct just because it is traditional. He was not urging people to abandon their traditions but rather to analyze whether or not the tradition was something that should continue or not in terms of the Buddhist lifestyle.

In general that would mean that as long as the tradition harmed no living being, and contributed to your happiness, you should continue to follow it.

Most traditional practises are centered around the search for enlightenment and, as a result, several different schools of Buddhism have appeared, each with a slightly different interpretation of the Buddha's message and how to incorporate it into life.

There are, however, some traditions that are common throughout all of these schools of thought.

## Pilgrimages

Making a pilgrimage to a shrine or holy site is an important part of the Buddhist tradition. The Buddha himself made several pilgrimages in India. Some pilgrims choose to follow the path of the Buddha, others choose to visit the more important sites such as visiting Buddha's birthplace in Lumbini or going to Sarnath, where Buddha gave his first sermon.

## Engaged Buddhism

Getting involved in helping others is another Buddhist tradition that is practised worldwide. The Buddha's message of compassion inspired a tradition of helping others. In fact, when you consider that in terms of Buddhist beliefs we are all connected to one another, it becomes hard to sit back and do nothing to help.

## Tea Ceremonies

Tea ceremonies are especially important in Zen Buddhism and follow very specific steps. They become an exercise in mindfulness for both those serving the tea and those who the tea is served to.

If you are privileged enough to be invited to a tea ceremony, be sure to attend - it is a true experience that is not quickly forgotten.

## Celebrations

Buddhism is in essence a celebration of life and so there are a lot of festivals and celebration worldwide. Buddhist New Year is one such joyful celebration and the date of the New Year depends on the calendar being followed - it is not ordinarily the 1st of January.

Buddhist celebrations tend to be full of light, color and noise.

# Chapter 8: Prayer and Rituals

## The Power of Prayer And Rituals

In Buddhism, no actual Gods or Goddesses are worshipped and so prayers take the form of meditations. During such meditations, a practitioner will often send light and love to others.

## The Most Important Part of Buddhist Prayer

Any time you meditate, the aim should be to be of pure mind. This is the most important part, especially when you are meditating for the benefit of others.

## Meditations to Aid Growth

You can meditate using visualizations in order to help your own spiritual or emotional state, or do so on behalf of others.

## The Sharing and Dedication of Merit

The best way to explain this is to compare it to a teacher who shares their knowledge with their students, except in this case the merits are spiritual.

The person meditating dedicates the lessons that he has learned to people he loves, people he knows or even strangers in order to help them benefit from the lessons as well. It is like sending out good vibes.

## Rituals

There are many different rituals when it comes to Buddhism and these will vary according to the area that you are in and the type of Buddhism that you practise. Fortunately, there is really no right or wrong in terms of Buddhism so you won't be penalized for saying the wrong words at the wrong time.

Most rituals are centered around making it easier to meditate anyway - whether it is in the use of prayer beads or bells.

As the Buddha himself said, the ritual/ tradition needs to make sense in your life. If you do not want to burn incense and wear an orange robe, don't. If this makes you happy, do it. You get to choose which rituals work for you in terms of your lifestyle. The choice really is yours.

That said, you should always be respectful of other people's rituals - remember that you must aim do no harm and be compassionate to everyone. This could mean simply standing quietly to one side while they go through the motions of the rituals that mean a lot to them.

# Chapter 9: Impermanence
## Because Nothing In This World Lasts

According to the Buddha, in order to attain enlightenment, we have to learn that nothing is permanent. We have to learn to let go of our attachments, whether that means to material things or whether that means to old grudges and outdated beliefs. All attachments are baggage that will weigh us down and hold us back.

## Bye Bye Material Things

Think back to your last Christmas or birthday. What gifts did you get? Can you even still remember? Most of us have this tendency to accumulate things - we buy things to celebrate, we buy things to help us feel better. Many of us are drowning in an ocean of stuff and it makes no difference how much we buy or are given, we always want more.

It is all such a huge waste. Think about how many hours a day you have to work to be able to afford all that stuff and it suddenly seems a lot less worthwhile.

## No Time for Grudges and Outdated Beliefs

So Susan at work stole your idea and pitched it to the boss? You'll probably be angry with her, you may even do something to get revenge on her. A few years down the line, will you even remember? Will it still be important or will there be something else to worry about?

There really is not a whole lot that goes on on a daily basis that is truly worth the time and effort that we spend worrying about it.

The more time you waste on these fruitless thoughts and actions, the less time you have to work towards achieving Nirvana.

## Constantly Striving for What?

We work hard and set goals - get a job, do well at it, get married, have kids, buy a house. You may have achieved some of those goals already. Do you feel happier and more fulfilled for it? Or do you spend a lot of time worrying about how you are going to maintain this lifestyle?

And what are you actually doing anyway? You are putting off life until some nebulous time in the future when you have achieved your goals, at the expense of the present.

In life, things will play out as they are meant to. Your soul needs to learn the lessons laid in front of it. That is why there is really no need to constantly strive to achieve goals.

# Chapter 10: Happiness, Fulfillment and Meaning

## Finding Your Purpose In Life

If you truly want to score points towards becoming more enlightened, finding out what lessons you have to learn in this incarnation and your life's purpose is really important. Anything else is simply just marking time until you die.

Think of life as a big school - if you don't learn your lesson, you have to repeat the year. The same applies with all of your lives. If you don't learn the lesson this time round, you have to give it another go in the next life and every life thereafter until the lesson is learned. And again, just like school, there is no graduation until all you have passed every year.

Do you really want to repeat the same lessons over and over again?

## Embrace Your Inner Child

Kids are a lot smarter than we give them credit for - how many times have you thought that you'd love to be a kid again? The truth is that a kid is basically a clean slate when it is born - yes, it does have a karmic background that governs the life it is born into, but it still looks at life in a completely different way.

Kids tend to live in the moment. It is only as they get older that they are taught to prepare for and worry about the future. They have a tendency to think that everything is possible and they can love at the drop of a hat. They don't worry that they will be rejected or that they will fail.

Clearly, we should be learning from them, instead of the other way round.

To find your true purpose in life, think back to when you were a kid. What things did you love doing? This is one of the best ways to get in touch with your true purpose in life. Would your younger self be pleased at the way you are living your life? What would they want to change?

## Analyze the Lessons Already Learned

This is a bit more difficult. We tend to look at the bad things in our life as mishaps when they are really lessons and ways to nudge us back onto the path we should be following with our lives.

I believe that one of the other life lessons I was put here to learn was how to let go of things and attachments. I'll explain briefly.

By the time I was 11, I had lost all my grandparents and also my father. My marriage broke up after 9 years. I had a job that I hated. I resigned from it and then went back, albeit to a different department. Then I went broke, and not just a little broke, I had to apply for debt counselling and agree not to enter into any more credit agreements. I lost my home and a lot of the stuff that I had accumulated over the years - Going through the clothes to see what could be sold, I found garments that had their price tags attached.

I then lost my job.

Okay, enough of a sob story for you?

I can honestly say that I am actually a very lucky person - going broke was the very best thing that could have happened to me. I would spend money like water and had very little to show for it at the end of the day. I now know the true value of a day's work.

I also believe that my experience has made me a much better person. I no longer care about wearing the right clothes or having the latest hair style. I now realize that those things can be taken away from you in a flash and actually mean nothing.

I found that I have a passion for helping others and love being able to make a living doing what I love, rather than just being a cog in a big, corporate machine.

I have learned that losing things is not worst thing in the world - I lost just about everything and I survived and thrived. Things are not important at all and never were.

## What are You Passionate About?

What is it that you love doing? Is there a way to make a living at it? Can you help others at the same time?

Finding your life's purpose is a lot easier than you think - you may even be surprised at what your purpose is, once you figure it out.

# Chapter 11: Karma
## What You Do Comes Back To You

Karma is a more complicated subject than we realize. Most of envisage the "eye for an eye" version we see in the Bible but this is simply not how karma works. It has much longer ranging effects than just one lifetime and it is not personal in the way that we believe it is.

What do you think that your next life will be like? The truth is probably that it will be very different from this one. You will not be you anymore - your personality, life circumstances, etc. will be completely different.

What karma will do, however, is to determine how much or how little you will suffer in your future incarnations. Consider karma to be the bank account - whenever you do good, a little interest is added. Whenever you do bad, funds are subtracted.

The purer your intentions and actions are in this life, the more good points you accumulate and the better your karma will be. Do bad things in this life, and you'll lose points and just invite more suffering into your future lives.

## Not Just One Lifetime

Another common misconception that people have is that karma only affects the lifetime directly following the one in which it was earned. The truth is that if you have enough good karma from previous lives, and this outweighs the bad you have done in this life, you could still have a fairly good rebirth.

The same is true of negative karma - bad deeds can affect not only in the very next incarnation but in the others following it is as well.

It simply really does not pay to lead an immoral life - always try to help your fellow man and try to act from the best intentions to keep karma in your favor.

# Chapter 12: Dharma

# The Natural Law And Human Suffering

It is said that when the Buddha presented his first sermon, he had no mystical texts or teachings to draw from - all he had was his own experience of the path, or dharma. From his experience he was able to determine the way to achieve enlightenment.

Dharma is, quite simply, everything - the natural laws in terms of human suffering, the way to achieve enlightenment as laid out by the Buddha and also all subsequent teachings as well.

Dharma is so much more than that as well - it can be anything that that helps you to awaken to the truth in life. Anything, or anyone, that tries to teach us what the truth is, is dharma - even those people in life who give us a really hard time.

Dharma is something that is hard to define because it can be anything.

Dharma is constantly changing and growing - it is something for you to use as and when you need it.

Dharma can mean different things to different people. Perhaps one person is awakened to the truth in the world when they heard a bird sing for the first time. For another person it may be seeing the sea for the first time or it may be something completely different.

# What Dharma Teaches Us

Dharma teaches us that it is important to be present and mindful in every moment of our lives. You never know when there is something that is going to help you see the truth in life and you need to be able to recognise it when it does.

Living in the present is the only way to pick up the lessons that life has to teach us now. If we are constantly living for the future, or living in the past, we are too distracted and may miss out on a lot of these truths.

# Chapter 13: Getting Started with Buddhism

## Ways To Start Your Own Journey To Enlightenment

Ready to get going on your own journey to enlightenment? Now is the best time to start - do not put it off a second longer.

Start by incorporating kind acts in your daily life, practising meditation and becoming more mindful in everything that you do.

Then get going on some more research - this book gives you an idea of what Buddhism involves but it is not a comprehensive resource. There is still a lot more to learn about Buddhism and many different schools of Buddhism as well.

By doing more research, you will be able to find which suits you best. Trust your instincts when choosing which school to follow.

Some of the concepts can be challenging to understand so don't give up easily and allow yourself time to fully understand what those concepts are.

It can also be helpful to join a group of like-minded people. Is there a Buddhist temple in the area or a group that you can join? The benefit of joining up is that you will have support when you need it. You can also draw on the experience of other group members as needed.

# Chapter 14: Further Resources
Resources To Help You Learn More

## Forums

http://www.buddhismwithoutboundaries.com/

http://www.freesangha.com/forums/

http://secularbuddhism.org/forum/

## Websites

http://www.quietmountain.org/buddhism.htm

http://www.tricycle.com/

## Cheat Sheets

http://www.dummies.com/how-to/content/mindfulness-for-dummies-cheat-sheet-uk-edition.html

http://www.dummies.com/how-to/content/meditation-for-dummies-cheat-sheet.html

http://www.womenshealthandfitness.com.au/health-beauty/health-advice/1442-meditation-for-beginners-tips

## Articles to Read

http://www.cheatsheet.com/life/5-ways-you-can-benefit-from-meditation.html/

http://www.parami.org/buddhistanswers/benefits_buddhism.htm

http://www.findingdulcinea.com/guides/Religion-and-Spirituality/Buddhism.pg_00.html

http://en.wikipedia.org/wiki/Buddhism

# Conclusion

I hope that you have found this book interesting and have developed a desire to learn more about Buddhism. All in all, Buddhism is more than just a different kind of religion - it is a complete lifestyle change.

The beauty of Buddhism is that your life is literally in your own hands and you are directly responsible for it. This is great as it means that your actions truly do determine your future.

Buddhism is a very gentle and tolerant lifestyle choice. There is no such thing as sin. As long as you aim to harm no living being and choose to act from moral intentions, you are on the right track.

As far as the main tenets of Buddhism go, they make sense for day to day living as well - have compassion for others, love them unconditionally and release your attachment to things.

If all of us could set aside our egos and work towards the betterment of our fellow man, this world would be a true utopia.

Go in light and love.

Printed in Great Britain
by Amazon